Make your own
cards

A Pyramid Craft Paperback

Make your own
cards

Petra Boase

hamlyn

An Hachette UK Company
www.hachette.co.uk

A Pyramid Paperback

First published in Great Britain in 2008 by
Hamlyn, a division of Octopus Publishing Group Ltd
2–4 Heron Quays, London E14 4JP
www.octopusbooks.co.uk
www.octopusbooksusa.com

Distributed in the U.S. and Canada by Octopus Books USA:
c/o Hachette Book Group USA
237 Park Avenue
New York NY 10017

This material was previously published as *Quick and Easy Handmade Cards*

ISBN 978-0-600-61810-2

A CIP catalogue record for this book is available
from the British Library

Printed and bound in China

10 9 8 7 6 5 4 3 2

Note
While the advice and information
in this book is believed to be
accurate, neither the author nor
the publisher will be responsible
for any injury, losses, damages,
actions, proceedings, claims,
demands, expenses and costs
(including legal costs or
expenses) incurred or in any
way arising out of following the
projects in this book.

Contents

introduction

Despite living in a fast-moving age of computer and mobile phone communication, there is still nothing more heart-warming than receiving a handmade greeting card, lovingly crafted by the sender. Making your own cards is hugely rewarding – not only is it a form of relaxation but it provides an outlet for your creativity and the end result is bound to be appreciated and treasured above any shop-bought card.

There are many occasions when a special, handmade card would be appreciated. The book is divided into three sections covering the most popular topics: Festive fun – dates such as Christmas and Easter, when it is traditional to send a card to mark the festivities; Celebrations – cards for those special moments such as a wedding or birth of a new baby; and Birthday – a selection of cards that can be adapted to suit any

birthday girl or boy. you just want to say hello or thank you. Handmade cards are the perfect choice for party invitations too, as you can personalize them with all the necessary details. Any of the cards in the book could be used in this way, but for thank-you notes and invitations you often need multiple copies – see Good luck horseshoe (see pages 90–93) as an example of a simple technique using linocutting that you can use.

The projects throughout the book are designed to kick start your imagination and show you a variety of simple card-making styles and techniques. Straightforward collage, appliqué, needlepoint, rubber stamping, papercrafting to create 3-D effects, wire work, and decoupage – all

techniques that can be easily achieved around the kitchen table in just a couple of hours.

All the basic techniques that are used in the projects are explained in the Tips and techniques section (see pages 16–19), with easy-to-follow photographs showing you how to transfer templates, cut out shapes and stencils, and finish your cards, including making and decorating envelopes. There is also a section on which tools you will need and how to use them (see pages 8–11), plus an overview of the materials that are required (see pages 12–15).

Art and craft stores are an Aladdin's cave of papers, tools and embellishments, and you can end up spending much more than you need. A list of equipment is provided to help get you started and soon you will find that a stock of paper, card, glue and a few decorations will provide the starting point for many imaginative ideas.

Ready-made card blanks, stickers, stamps and pre-cut shapes are all available but by looking closer to home you will produce individual cards that have your own personal touch, at half the price. Be creative and look around for everyday items, such as old scraps of fabric, paper, even wallpaper, with which to decorate your cards. Old photographs, magazine cuttings, pressed flowers – all can be used to give your card an individual twist. Many of the projects use

scraps of fabric and ribbon to great effect – see Baby patchwork (see pages 66–9), Polka dot present (see pages 124–27) and Button flower (see pages 120–23) for some ideas. Drawing an original design or pattern can be a stumbling block and that is why the templates of all the motifs on the cards are provided at actual size, so that you can get started straight away.

All the cards can be personalized in different ways to make them unique to you – choose an alternative colour theme or a different-sized card; mix and match templates or motifs; or adapt the pattern or shapes. Simplicity is the key, and if you bear in mind that 'less is more', you will produce stylish, individual cards to be proud of.

Good luck!

tools

The great thing about paper craft is that you don't need to invest in lots of expensive, technical equipment. For general card making a craft knife, cutting mat, ruler, pair of scissors and pot of PVA glue will be sufficient to get you started. There are some techniques that require more specialist equipment, such as jewellery pliers or lino cutters, and it is worth investing in these as and when required.

cutting out

Invest in a good pair of general scissors, together with a smaller pair for cutting fabric and threads. Never use your fabric scissors for cutting card as this will blunt them. For cutting windows or intricate patterns a craft knife and cutting mat are essential.

Craft knife (scalpel) This is an invaluable tool when making greeting cards. Choose a knife where you can replace the blades or snap them off to ensure that your blade is always sharp; this is important for clean cutting lines. Rotary cutters are good for card and fabric. Use with a cutting mat to protect your work surface from cuts and scratches, and with a metal edge ruler to ensure a straight line and safe cutting.

Craft scissors These are good all round scissors for cutting paper, card and other craft materials.

Cutting mat A rubberized, self-healing mat to be used when cutting paper, card or fabric with a craft knife to protect work surfaces. Mats are available in different sizes (from A1 to A5) and many feature a useful grid for keeping your angles square.

Embroidery scissors Small scissors used for finer sewing projects and cutting threads.

Fabric scissors Sharp scissors used for cutting fabric. Do not use for cutting paper or card as they will soon become blunt.

Lino cutter and blades Use for cutting into lino to make a print block. Different size blades are fixed into the handle one at a time to create different cuts of varying depth and width in the lino, such as a fine blade for cutting intricate details.

Paper punch Patterned paper punches are available in a range of shapes and can be used on paper and card. Border and corner punches are also available. A simple hole punch can also be used for creating perfect dots.

Patterned scissors Scissors with patterned blades are readily available from craft shops and haberdashers. These give you the option of cutting fabric or card with a patterned edge, such as scalloped, wavy and deckle. For a zigzag effect you can use the classic pinking shears.

general tools

Keep a pencil, ruler and eraser to hand in your craft box alongside your cutting equipment, as these tools are all invaluable

Cutting tools and roller

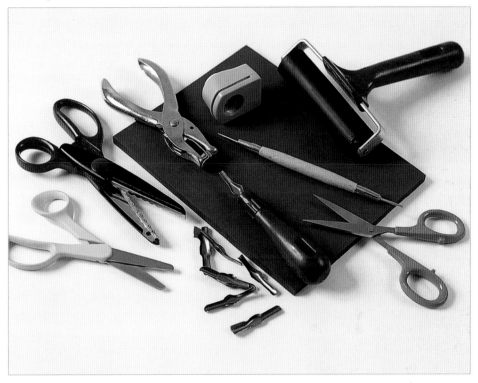

for marking and measuring cards, templates and decorations.

Embossing tool and mat Similar to a pen, this tool has a rounded end that is used for embossing shapes on special parchment paper or metal foil. It is also useful for scoring the crease of cards before folding them in half. Use with a soft embossing mat.

Eraser This is useful for erasing any pencil lines you have used. A smooth-edge eraser

can also be used to make a rubber stamp; choose one that is large enough to take your chosen design and can be handled easily.

Face mask This should be worn when using spray adhesive or spray paint to protect you from inhaling the fumes.

Metal edge ruler Use with a craft knife or scalpel, along with a ruler if cutting a straight line, to ensure that you cut an even edge and to prevent the blade from slipping.

Pencil A sharp pencil is useful for marking measurements or positions; use a soft pencil, such as a 2B, if you need to erase the mark. Use a harder HB pencil for tracing outlines and drawing around templates.

Ruler A long, clear ruler is essential for measuring pieces of paper and finding the centre of the card before folding.

Tweezers These are useful for picking up and placing small sequins or beads, and for applying gold leaf.

specialist tools

These tools are not essential basic equipment but are worth investing in if you wish to expand your range of techniques and your creative scope.

Flower press Place fresh flowers and leaves between the layers of paper and card and do up tightly.

Jewellery pliers These pliers have a smaller point than normal tools and are easier to use in craft projects.

Specialist tools

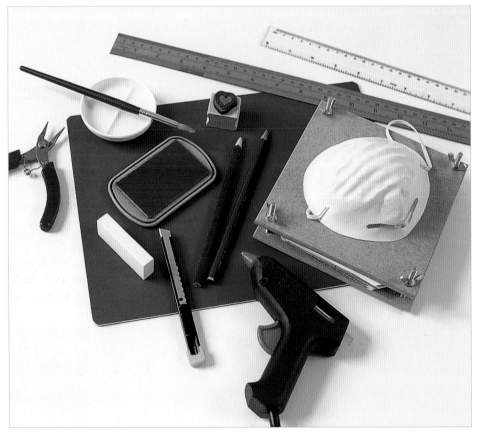

Rubber covered roller (brayer) Use when making lino prints for spreading ink on the glass surface and applying ink to the lino cut before making a print.

sticking equipment

Many brands of PVA glue are available with an integral brush or a nozzle for accurate application but you will find a separate brush useful for applying large areas of glue and for following a shape or stencil.

Glue brush A basic painting brush to apply PVA water-based glue. Wash after each use.

Glue gun A very useful tool for when you want glue to dry quickly or for sticking small, fiddly items. Hot glue guns should be handled with care.

paper

Paper and card are the basic ingredients for any card-making project. Available in a rainbow of colours and tones, plain or patterned, textured or metallic, thick or thin, the choice is endless. In addition to this huge choice is the range of handmade papers, with different colours and textures, some with additions such as petals or leaves. If you have time, you can also make your own paper.

Paper sizes vary but there are standard sheet sizes available such as:

A4 (290 x 297 mm/8¼ x 11¹¹⁄₁₆ in)

A5 (148 x 210 mm /5⅚ x 8¼ in)

These have been used for the projects.

Larger sheets of some papers can be purchased and cut down as required. When choosing paper or card, select a thickness or weight that will fold easily and remain rigid (such as 230–260 gsm). The weight of paper and card is measured in grams per square metre (gsm).

Acetate An opaque, thin sheet of plastic that can be drawn or photocopied onto.

Drawing paper Use a thin, plain white paper for copying templates and patterns.

Card Many of the projects use standard A4 or A5 sheets of card for the folded card blank.

Lino board Used for cutting into to make the base for a lino print.

Thick card Useful for making stencils.

Thin card This is ideal for making templates which need to be flexible but rigid enough to stay in place when drawing around the edges of the design.

Tissue paper Available in a range of colours, this is ideal for adding delicate details or layering, or mounted behind a window or cut-out for a stained glass effect.

Tracing paper Useful for copying and transferring templates.

Translucent paper Parchment or vellum paper has an opaque quality and is available in many colours and patterns. It can be used for embossing or decoration.

Wallpaper Leftover rolls of old wallpaper, especially those with a clear pattern, make a great starting place for collage cards.

materials

After paper and card, the other materials that you require for handmade cards will very much depend on the style and techniques of the project. For most cards you will need a reliable form of adhesive, be it PVA glue, adhesive tape, spray adhesive or sticky foam pads. Your other materials – from fabric scraps and buttons to craft wire and ink pads – can be acquired separately for each project.

adhesives

Art and craft stores stock an amazing array of different adhesives, but with a pot of PVA glue, a can of spray adhesive and some sticky tape you will be able to assemble most handmade cards.

Adhesive foam pads These are double-sided sticky pads that are very useful when you want part of your design to be raised slightly from the background.

Range of adhesives

Embossing powder

Adhesive tape A general tape is useful for sticking backgrounds or securing shapes that will be hidden from view.

Double-sided adhesive tape This tape comes in different widths and is invaluable for sticking down paper or card cut-outs, frames, background panels and collage pieces. Simply peel off the backing paper and smooth down in place. Note: It cannot be repositioned.

Heat adhesive webbing An iron-on webbing used in simple appliqué projects to help stick fabric shapes in place on a background fabric before sewing in position.

PVA glue A versatile, water based, slow-drying adhesive. It sticks paper, card, fabric, buttons, and sequins.

Spray adhesive Available in a spray can that produces a fine spray of adhesive that covers the whole surface with an even layer. It is a quick way of sticking paper and fabric shapes in place and allows for a little repositioning. Cover your surface with newspaper before applying the spray.

Note: Spray adhesive is highly-flammable and toxic. Always use in a well-ventilated area and avoid contact with skin and eyes. Wear a face mask and avoid inhaling the vapour.

decorations

From tiny beads to embossed rubber stamps, your choice of decoration is almost endless. Each project in this book suggests the materials to use. However, as you build up your supply you can choose your own and be even more creative.

Beads and buttons Available from haberdashers and craft stores, these make very versatile decorations, from tiny beads to character buttons, all in different shapes, sizes and colours.

Craft wire This comes in different widths (gauges) and colour finishes. Use with a pair of jewellery pliers to bend the wire into different shapes.

Embossing metal A soft craft metal that is easy to cut with scissors or a craft knife. You can impress a pattern onto the metal using an old ballpoint pen or special embossing tool.

Embossing powder This fine powder is available in many colours and needs to be used in conjunction with a binder, such as ink from a rubber stamp. Stamp a shape on the card and sprinkle on the powder, shake off the excess and hold over a heat source until the powder melts to form the shape. Crafter's heat guns are available.

Glitter Available in a wide range of colours and sizes from heavy to fine.

Gold leaf A very thin sheet of gold leaf that can be applied to an adhesive background with a brush.

Sequins Available in standard, plain sizes but also in flower and novelty shapes to suit different occasions.

pens, paints and inks

A selection of coloured pencils or paints is always good to have close at hand for adding finishing touches.

Coloured pencils These are ideal for adding hand-drawn details on cards or for filling in colours on rubber stamp designs.

Fabric marker pen This is useful when drawing around templates onto fabric as they don't bleed outside the edges of the design like some standard markers.

Gutta This is a liquid resist used in silk painting to outline the design. Once dry it acts as a barrier to the silk paint to prevent the colour bleeding outside the edges of the design.

Dye stamping ink Dye inks produce the most vibrant colours and work on all sorts of papers and even fabrics. You can buy refills when your ink pad runs dry.

Pigment stamping ink A slower drying ink that resembles paint. Use pigment stamping ink on matt, porous paper.

Lino printing ink Available in water- or oil-based varieties. The water-based is quick to dry and easy to clean.

Silk paints These come in many vibrant colours and can be mixed to create more tones. Apply with a fine paintbrush.

fabrics

Scrap pieces of fabric, felts and wools look very effective on a handmade card. With the addition of ribbon, lace and some simple stitching you can really make the most of all those odds and ends at the bottom of your sewing basket.

Using ribbon for detail

Patterns and plains A cotton or cotton/ polyester mix fabric is best for cutting out without the risk of the edges fraying. Dress fabric, upholstery fabric and craft fabrics are all suitable. Fabrics with a large pattern are ideal for cutting round for appliqué shapes.

Felt This is a soft but dense material that is easy to cut and shape and is available in a range of colours. For a thicker, more handmade effect, wash the felt in a washing machine: some shrinkage may occur.

Lace This is very effective on its own or used as a stencil to recreate the pattern in ink or paint.

Ribbons There are many textures, colours and patterns available which will enhance any card design.

Silk A shiny surface that is not easy to cut into specific shapes but makes a good background for painting in conjunction with a gutta resist liquid.

Threads Cotton, wool and silk threads are useful for adding stitched decorations to a card or finishing appliqué pieces.

Wool Similar to felt but more delicate, wool gives a very soft effect perfect for baby cards.

tips and techniques

These basic techniques will help you to transfer motifs onto card to make templates or stencils, show you how to create a card blank with a neat crease, detail how to make a lino cut and explain simple appliqué stitches. There are also tips on making and decorating envelopes to finish your cards with style.

making a template

1 Draw over the outlines of the template on a sheet of tracing paper with a soft pencil.

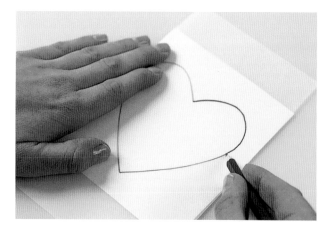

2 Turn the tracing paper over and scribble pencil marks on the reverse over the traced image.

3 Place the tracing paper scribbled side down on a piece of thin card and draw over the outlines again to transfer the design.

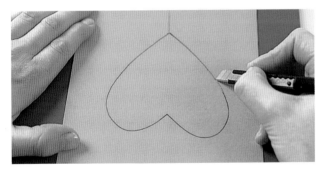

4 Remove the tracing paper to reveal the shape and cut out the template using scissors or a craft knife.

making a stencil

1 Trace and transfer the design as described in 'Making a template' (see left), onto thick card or plastic.

2 Using a craft knife and cutting mat, carefully cut around the edges of the design and remove the card to reveal the shape.

3 To use the stencil, place over your card and fix in place either with spray adhesive or masking tape. You can apply paint, glue or spray paint to the stencil.

4 When the paint or glue is tacky, carefully remove the stencil to reveal the design.

folding a card

making a linocut

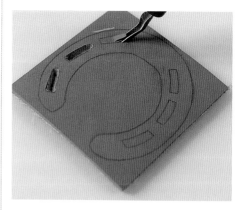

1 Cut out the piece of card to the required size. Use a ruler to divide the card in half and mark the centre points with an embossing tool. Alternatively, line up the centre with a gridline on your cutting mat.

(see Good luck horseshoe, pages 90–93)

1 Mark the design on the lino with a pencil by either transferring a template trace direct or by drawing around a template.

2 With the embossing tool and a ruler, draw a line joining the embossed marks and fold the card in half. If you don't have an embossing tool, the back of a table knife or a bone folder will also score the card. For a neat crease, run a metal spoon along the edge.

2 To make cutting into the lino easier, warm the lino by leaving it on a radiator for 5 minutes or outside on a sunny day. Position the lino up against a wall or firm edge as this will prevent slipping when you cut out the lino. Score around the design with a craft knife.

3 Use different width blades in a lino cutter, such as a wide blade for cutting out large areas and a fine blade for more detailed areas, and cut out the design. The linocut is now ready to be inked for printing.

appliqué stitches

You can secure fabric pieces to card with spray adhesive or PVA glue, but to complete the card with a decorative finish you can't beat these simple, traditional stitches.

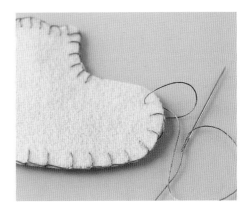

Blanket stitch (top right) Hold the side that you are working on towards you. Starting from the left, bring the needle up through the fabric so that it catches the edge and is pointing towards you. Loop the thread over the needle then make the next stitch by bringing the needle back through the fabric approximately 5 mm (⅛ in) to the right. Continue working left to right along the edge of the fabric.

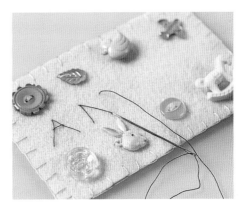

Running stitch (centre right) Thread your needle with a length of embroidery thread or cotton. Take four or five even stitches together, then gently pull the thread through the fabric before taking another series of stitches.

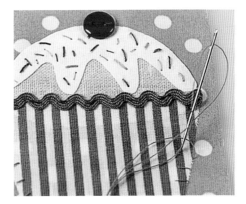

Slip stitch (below right) Work from right to left along the folded edge of the fabric. Bring the needle up through the folded edge and back down into the background fabric at a slight angle. Bring the needle back up again about 5 mm (⅛ in) down from the previous stitch, through the folded edge and continue stitching at regular intervals.

making an envelope

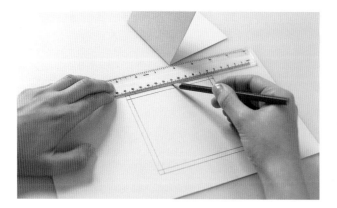

1 Make a template of your card by measuring out the finished, folded size on a piece of thin card, adding about 5 mm (⅛ in) to each edge. This is the front of the envelope.

2 Next, add the top flap on the upper edge, measuring half the depth of the front. Add the back on the lower edge, measuring the full size of the finished card, less about 2 cm (¾ in).

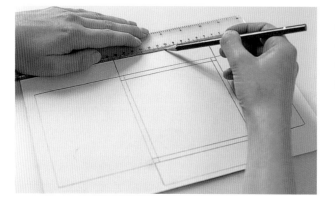

3 Add the side folds to each outer edge of the front, measuring 2.5 cm (1 in) wide. You can round off the corners if you prefer.

4 Cut out the template using sharp scissors and draw around it on your chosen paper or card. Fold the back and top flaps into the centre and the side folds inwards.

5 Open out the flaps and either apply a thin layer of PVA glue to the side flaps or a strip of double-sided tape and seal the edges. Either tuck the top flap in or seal with double-sided tape or a fun sticker.

festive fun

Traditional festivities and celebrations give you the opportunity to make special handmade cards for family and friends. In this section you will find a broad selection of Christmas-themed cards that will suit all ages, together with hand-painted silk eggs or a cute fluffy bunny for Easter greetings. The cards use simple collage and 3-D effects together with glitter and gold leaf which are perfect for seasonal greetings.

bobbing snowmen

These plump little snowmen are attached
to the card background with a wire spiral,
so that they can spring forwards and merrily
bob up and down.

materials

1 A5 sheet of deep purple card

1 sheet of A5 white card

1 sheet of pink metallic card (for a hat)

1 sheet of gold paper (for a hat and scarf)

assorted small coloured sequins

snowflake rubber stamp

white ink pad

white embossing powder

PVA glue

20-cm (8-in) length of jewellery wire

fine tip black pen

equipment

scissors

toaster

pencil

glue gun

to make the **bobbing snowmen** card

1 Fold the purple card in half and open out
flat. Stamp the snowflake design all over
the card with white ink. Re-apply ink to the
stamp for each print.

2 Sprinkle the white embossing powder
over each stamped snowflake and shake
off the excess. Immediately hold the stamped
snowflakes over a heat source, such as a
toaster, until the powder melts.

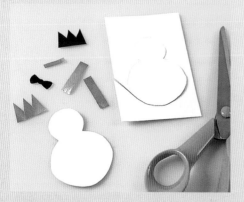

3 Trace the snowmen templates onto
white card and cut them out. Cut out the
shapes for the hat, bow tie and scarf from the
different coloured papers.

4 With a dab of PVA glue, stick the hats,
scarf and sequins onto the snowmen.
Draw the facial details with a black fine tip pen

5 Cut the length of wire in half. Coil each piece around a pencil to make a spiral. Glue one end of the wire to the reverse of the snowman just below the head with a hot glue gun. Glue a small piece of white card over the fixing point. Repeat for the second snowman.

6 Decide where you want to position the snowmen and mark the spot with a pencil. Apply a generous amount of glue from a hot gun, glue to the spot and then attach the wire. Support the wire while the glue dries. Repeat for the second snowman.

spinning star

The origami papers used in this design create an optical effect as the star spins. You can use any patterned papers in a common colour theme.

materials

1 A5 sheet of red card

1 A4 sheet of thin card

1 sheet of striped paper
(10.5 x 15 cm/4¼ x 7½ in)

PVA glue

1 sheet of red card
(15 x 15 cm/6 x 6 in)

2 sheets of different
patterned origami paper
(15 x 15 cm/6 x 6 in)

red thread

adhesive tape

equipment

pencil

scissors

craft knife

cutting mat

glue brush

fabric scissors

needle

to make the **spinning star** card

 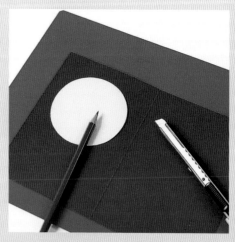

1 Fold the red card in half. Photocopy or trace the star and circle templates onto the thin card and cut out with scissors.

2 Position the circle template on the inside front of the card, approximately 2.5 cm (1 in) from the top, and draw around with a pencil. Cut out the circle with a craft knife.

3 Apply PVA glue to the inside right-hand page of the card and stick the piece of striped paper on top.

4 Stick the patterned paper squares to each side of the square of red card with PVA glue.

5 Position the star template in the centre of the patterned square and trace with a pencil. Cut out the star with a craft knife.

6 Thread the needle with a length of red thread and attach the star to the round window by piercing a hole in the top point of the star and again at the top of the circle in the red card. Secure the thread with adhesive tape.

3-D snow scene

With a few simple folds and some adhesive
tape, this 3-D card is easy to assemble.
You could add snowmen in place of the
trees for variation.

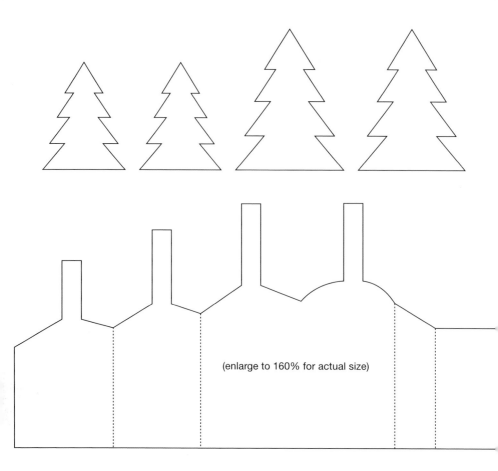

(enlarge to 160% for actual size)

materials

1 A5 sheet of blue card

1 A5 sheet of thin white card

1 A5 sheet of thin green
  metallic card

silver glitter

white fine glitter

PVA glue

double-sided tape

equipment

pencil

old ballpoint pen or
  embossing tool

glue brush

snowflake paper punch

scissors

to make the **3-D snow scene** card

 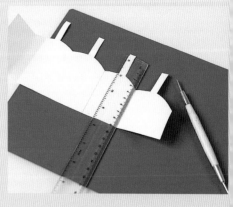

1 Fold the blue card in half. Photocopy or trace the snow scene and Christmas tree templates. Draw around the snow scene template on the white card and the Christmas trees on the green card, then cut out.

2 Score along the fold lines on the snow scene (see template) with an old ballpoint pen or embossing tool and fold them back.

3 Glue the Christmas trees onto the tabs of the snow scene using a small dab of PVA glue.

4 Brush PVA glue over the white card and sprinkle on the silver glitter, avoiding the tab on the far right. Shake off the excess.

5 Attach a strip of double-sided tape on the reverse of the left-hand side of the snow scene, another strip on the reverse side along the inside edge of the first fold, and one strip along the front edge of the last fold. Attach to the blue card.

6 Punch out white card snowflakes and brush with PVA glue. Sprinkle the snowflakes with white glitter, then shake off the excess and leave to dry.

7 Glue the snowflakes on the inside of the blue card behind the snow scene, and a few on the outside.

silk painted eggs

Silk paints are easy to apply and allow you
the freedom to add your own exclusive design.
When using these paints you first apply gutta,
a liquid resist that, once dry, acts as a barrier
to prevent the colour bleeding.

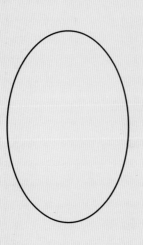

materials

1 sheet of lilac card
   (30 x 9 cm/12 x 3½ in)
1 A4 sheet of thin card
1 sheet of lilac card
   (15 x 9 cm/6 x 3½ in)
piece of white silk
   (15 x 7.5 cm/6 x 3 in)
1 sheet of thin card
   (16 x 12 cm/6¼ x 4¾ in)

gutta/resist fluid in pink and
   gold
silk paint in different colours
masking tape
double-sided tape

equipment

craft knife
cutting mat
pencil
paint brush

to make the **silk painted eggs** card

1 Fold the larger piece of lilac card in half. Photocopy or trace the egg template and cut out from the piece of thin card.

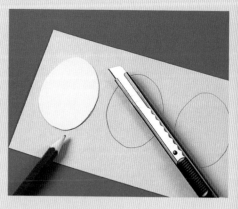

2 Draw around the egg template on the reverse of the front of the lilac card to make a row of three eggs. Cut out the eggs with a craft knife.

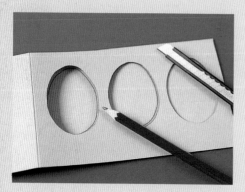

3 Place the smaller piece of lilac card behind the eggs and draw the outline of the eggs on the lilac card with a pencil, then cut out the eggs. The stencil shape will be added later to conceal the surrounding silk inside the card.

4 Tape the piece of silk to the slightly larger piece of thin card. Place the greeting card over the silk and very lightly draw around the eggs with a pencil onto the silk.

5 Outline the egg designs by applying the pink gutta/resist tube tip in a sufficiently thick and continuous line. Use the gutta/resist to outline patterns and shapes in pink and gold. Allow to dry for at least an hour.

6 Paint each colour of silk paint onto the chosen area of the design – rinse and dry the brush well in between colours. You can re-apply colours to create deeper tones. Allow the paint to dry for one hour.

7 Remove the silk from the backing card. Tape the design behind the egg windows with masking tape. To finish, stick the lilac backing card stencil over the reverse of the design with double-sided tape.

pom-pom bunny

This sweet Easter bunny will appeal to adults and children alike. Vary the colours or increase the number of bunnies for an alternative design.

materials

1 A5 sheet of yellow card

1 sheet of thin card (10.5 x 10.5 cm/4½ x 4½ in)

1 piece of pink and white spot fabric 10.5 x 10.5 cm/4½ x 4½ in)

spray adhesive

scraps of fabric for the bunting

PVA glue

adhesive foam pads

pink pom-pom

equipment

small scissors

pencil

glue brush

coloured pencil

glue gun

to make the **pom-pom bunny** card

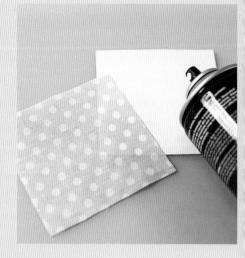

1 Fold the yellow card in half. Cut out a square of thin card and fabric (10.5 x 10.5 cm/4½ x 4½ in).

2 Spray adhesive over the front of the thin card and smooth the fabric on top.

3 Photocopy or trace the bunny and bunting templates and cut them out. Trace around the bunny template on the reverse of the spotty fabric and cut out with small scissors. Trace around the bunting template on four scraps of fabric and cut them out.

4 Glue the bunting in place along the top of the card and draw a coloured pencil line to link them together.

5 Apply two adhesive pads on the reverse of the bunny and stick onto the card. Fix the pom-pom tail with a hot glue gun.

celebrations

Engagement, wedding, new baby, new home, anniversary,

Mother's Day and Father's Day – all great excuses for making a

card and joining in the celebrations. The cards in this section use

a variety of techniques, from a layered fabric wedding cake to appliqué

felt shapes, and simple wire work with stylish embellishments.

For stitchers, the needlepoint house is an unusual idea with which

to welcome friends to a new home. The Father's Day card can be

adapted to suit any occasion and the patterned love heart lends itself

to St Valentine's day, engagement,wedding or anniversary wishes.

wedding cake

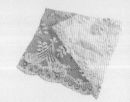

You can always add a personal touch to this design by writing the name of the couple and the date of their special day on the card.

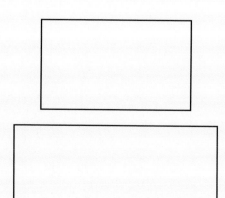

materials

1 sheet of cream card
(30 x 15 cm/12 x 6 in)

1 A4 sheet of thin card

1 sheet of pale pink tracing
paper (13 x 13 cm/5 x 5 in)

spray adhesive

1 sheet of thick white card
(13 x 13 cm/5 x 5 in)

13-cm (5-in) square of old
pink cotton lace fabric

20-cm (8-in) length of old
pink lace trim

double-sided tape

PVA glue

16 gold sequins

2 white dove cake
decorations

equipment

scissors

pencil

ruler

glue gun

to make the **wedding cake** card

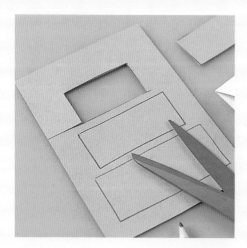

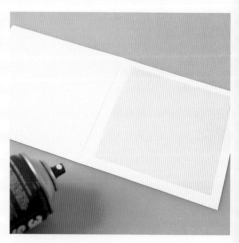

1 Fold the cream card in half. Trace or photocopy the cake templates onto thin card and cut out.

2 Spray adhesive on the reverse of the tracing paper and fix in the centre on the front of the card.

3 Spray adhesive on the thick white card and, when tacky, smooth on the lace fabric.

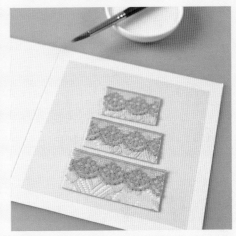

4 Draw around the cake templates on the lace card and cut out. Cut lengths of lace trim to fit each shape and attach with a thin strip of double-sided tape.

5 Glue the cake pieces onto the greeting card with a 5-mm (⅛-in) gap in between each layer.

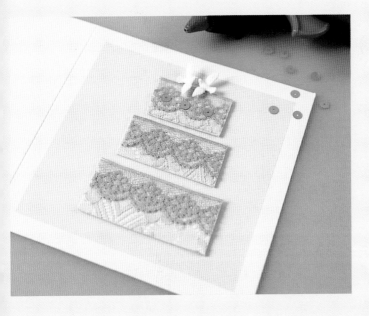

6 To finish, glue the sequins onto the cake pieces and glue the doves onto the top tier of the cake with a hot glue gun.

confetti church

This design can be adapted in many ways: you could use real confetti or dried rose petals; or vary the window shape – a heart or wedding cake would look perfect too.

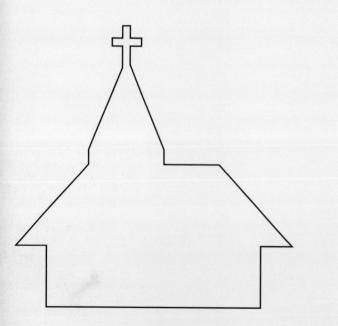

materials

1 A5 sheet of white card

1 A4 sheet of thin card

1 sheet of lilac card
  (10.5 x 15 cm/4¼ x 6 in)

1 A5 sheet of acetate

selection of small novelty
  sequins

masking tape

double-sided adhesive tape

equipment

cutting mat

craft knife

scissors

pencil

to make the **confetti church** card

1 Fold the white card in half. Trace or photocopy the church template onto thin card and cut out.

2 Place the church template on the inside of the front of the card and draw around it.

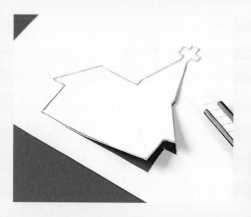

3 Cut out the church with a craft knife on a cutting mat.

4 Place the piece of lilac card behind the church and draw the outline of the church onto the lilac card, then cut out the church shape with a craft knife. This will be added later to finish off the card.

5 Cut out two pieces of acetate measuring 10 x 11.5 cm (4 x 4¾ in). Tape the two pieces together with masking tape leaving one side open. Fill the acetate pocket with the sequins and secure the open end with masking tape.

6 Fix the acetate pocket to the inside of the card behind the cut-out church with double-sided tape. To finish the card, stick the lilac church cut-out behind the church with double-sided tape.

diamond ring

This is an engagement card with extra sparkle! For a wedding card, simply use the gold band and add a hand-written message in metallic gold ink.

materials

1 A5 sheet of stencil card
1 sheet of pale pink card
   (21 x 10.5 cm/8¼ x 4¼ in)
spray adhesive
silver glitter
tiny gold beads
PVA glue

equipment

pencil
craft knife
cutting mat
glue brush
scissors
pencil

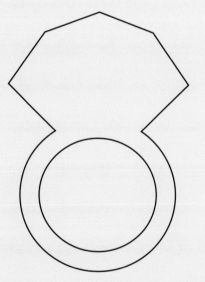

to make the **diamond ring** card

1 Trace the ring template onto stencil card and cut out with a craft knife to make the stencil. Keep the centre of the ring.

2 Fold the pink card in half. Spray adhesive on the reverse of the stencil and the centre of the ring and position both stencils on the front of the card.

3 With the glue brush, apply a generous amount of PVA glue to the reverse side of the stencil ring shape.

4 Carefully sprinkle the silver glitter so that it sticks to the jewel part of the ring. Lightly press down.

5 Apply more glue and sprinkle the beads over the band part of the ring then shake off the excess beads and glitter. Leave to dry for approximately half an hour.

6 Carefully remove the stencils to reveal the sparkling ring.

lace heart

Stamping and stencilling your own designs onto paper, card and even ribbon is very satisfying and produces a card that is unique to you.

materials

1 A5 sheet of pink card

1 A4 sheet of thin white card

1 sheet of red card
(10 x 10 cm/4 x 4 in)

1 piece of lace
(10 x 10 cm/4 x 4 in)

pink spray paint

36-cm (15-in) length of cotton ribbon tape

spot shape rubber stamp

rubber stamp ink pads in pink and deep pink

adhesive foam pads

spray adhesive

equipment

scissors

pencil

ruler

glue gun

(enlarge to 130% for actual size)

to make the **lace heart** card

1 Fold the pink card in half. Trace or photocopy the heart template onto thin card and cut out.

2 Spray adhesive on the reverse of the lace and smooth down on the red card. Spray pink paint through the lace. Allow to dry for 5 minutes and remove the lace.

3 Stamp spots onto one side of the cotton tape ribbon with a deep pink ink.

4 Stamp pink spots all over the background card, front and back.

5 Trace around the heart template on the stencilled red card and cut out the heart shape.

6 Tie the ribbon in a bow and it glue onto the heart.

7 Stick the heart on the spotty card using adhesive foam pads to raise the heart away from the design and give a 3-D effect.

baby bootee

The perfect new baby card. Here, the baby's
initial is stamped on the little tag, but you
could write the baby's full name instead.
For a little girl's version use pink tones.

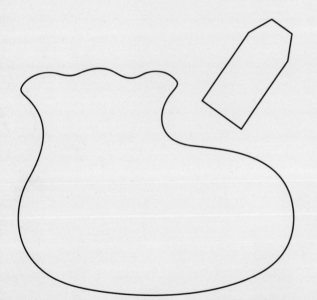

materials

1 sheet of cream card
   (30 x 15 cm/12 x 6 in)

1 A4 sheet of thin card

cream wool or felt
   (10 x 10 cm/4 x 4 in)

fine blue embroidery thread

8-cm (3-in) length of blue
   ribbon

pale blue card for the tag
   (3 x 2 cm/1½ x 1 in)

alphabet rubber stamps

blue ink pad

cream button

patterned paper
   (10 x 9 cm/4 x 3¾ in)

PVA glue

equipment

pencil

scissors

fabric scissors

needle

ruler

glue gun

glue brush

to make the **baby bootee** card

1 Fold the cream card in half. Trace or photocopy the bootie and tag templates onto thin card and cut them out.

2 Trace around the bootie template on the cream wool and carefully cut out with fabric scissors.

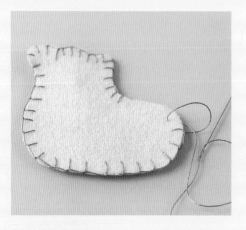

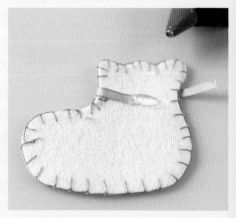

3 Blanket stitch (see page 19) around the edge of the bootee using the blue embroidery thread.

4 Wrap the ribbon around the top of the bootee and glue in place on the reverse with a glue gun.

5 Cut out the tag from the pale blue card and, using a rubber stamp, stamp on the baby's initial.

6 Glue the tag onto the front of the bootee and glue on the button with a hot glue gun.

7 Cut out the patterned paper for the background and glue it onto the card with PVA glue. Finally, glue on the bootie with a hot glue gun.

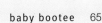

baby patchwork

A personalized welcome to the world. This delightful card uses simple stitches and would suit newborn baby wishes or a christening or naming ceremony.

materials

1 A5 sheet of mint green card

1 sheet of thin card
  (10.5 x 15 cm/4¼ x 6 in)

1 A5 piece of cream felt

assorted cotton threads

assorted buttons and sequins

double-sided tape

equipment

pencil

ruler

scissors

needle

to make the **baby patchwork** card

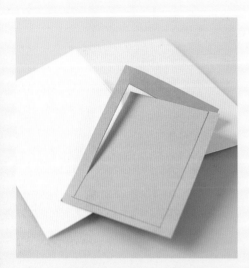

1 Fold the sheet of white card in half. Cut out a rectangle of thin card, 7 x 10.5 cm (3 x 4¼ in). You may have to adjust the sizes of the pieces of card according to how many letters the baby's name has.

2 Trace around the card rectangle on the felt and cut out with scissors.

3 Thread the needle with blue thread and blanket stitch (see page 19) around the edge of the piece of felt.

4 Attach the buttons and sequins with thread in two rows along the top and bottom of the felt rectangle.

5 With pink thread, use simple stitches to add the baby's name, keeping the letters evenly spaced.

6 Attach the felt panel to the card with double-sided tape.

new home

Modelling clay is ideal for simple decorations and is available in a huge range of colours, together with pretty pearlescent and fun glow-in-the-dark varieties.

materials

1 A5 sheet of green card

modelling clay in two colours, such as white and silver

1 A5 sheet of bronze paper

PVA glue

1 A4 sheet of white paper

bird charms or sequins

equipment

small rolling pin

oven

glue gun

glue brush

craft knife

to make the **new home** card

1 Fold the green card in half. Roll out a small ball of silver modelling clay the size of a walnut with a small rolling pin, until it is approximately 5 mm (⅛ in) thick. This is the background.

2 Roll another small ball of clay in the second colour into a continuous, thin rolled strip, until it is approximately 5 mm (⅛ in) thick.

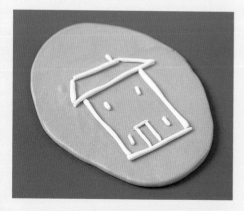

3 Cut the rolled strip into different length pieces to make up the shape of a house. Position the strips on the clay background and press down lightly.

4 Working in one direction only, roll over the design with the small rolling pin – the house shape will sink into the background clay to make a smooth surface.

5 Cut around the outline of the house leaving a narrow border of the background colour

6 Bake the clay shape following the instructions on the clay packet. Once baked and cooled, stick the house onto the folded card background with a hot glue gun.

7 Make a fence from thin strips of bronze paper and attach with PVA glue. Trace the cloud template onto white paper and cut out. Attach the cloud and bird charms to the sky with PVA glue to finish the card.

new home   73

needlepoint house

This is the perfect portable project to do in the evenings, on your travels or simply while chatting to friends.

materials

interlock canvas 12 count
  (13 x 13 cm/5¼ x 5¼ in)

sheet of tracing paper

tapestry wool in green, grey,
  brown, pink, turquoise,
  yellow

1 sheet of blue card
  (30 x 15 cm/12 x 7½ in)

1 sheet of blue card
  (15 x 15 cm/7½ x 7½ in)

masking tape

double-sided tape

equipment

tapestry needle

cutting mat

craft knife

metal edge ruler

scissors

(enlarge to 150% for actual size)

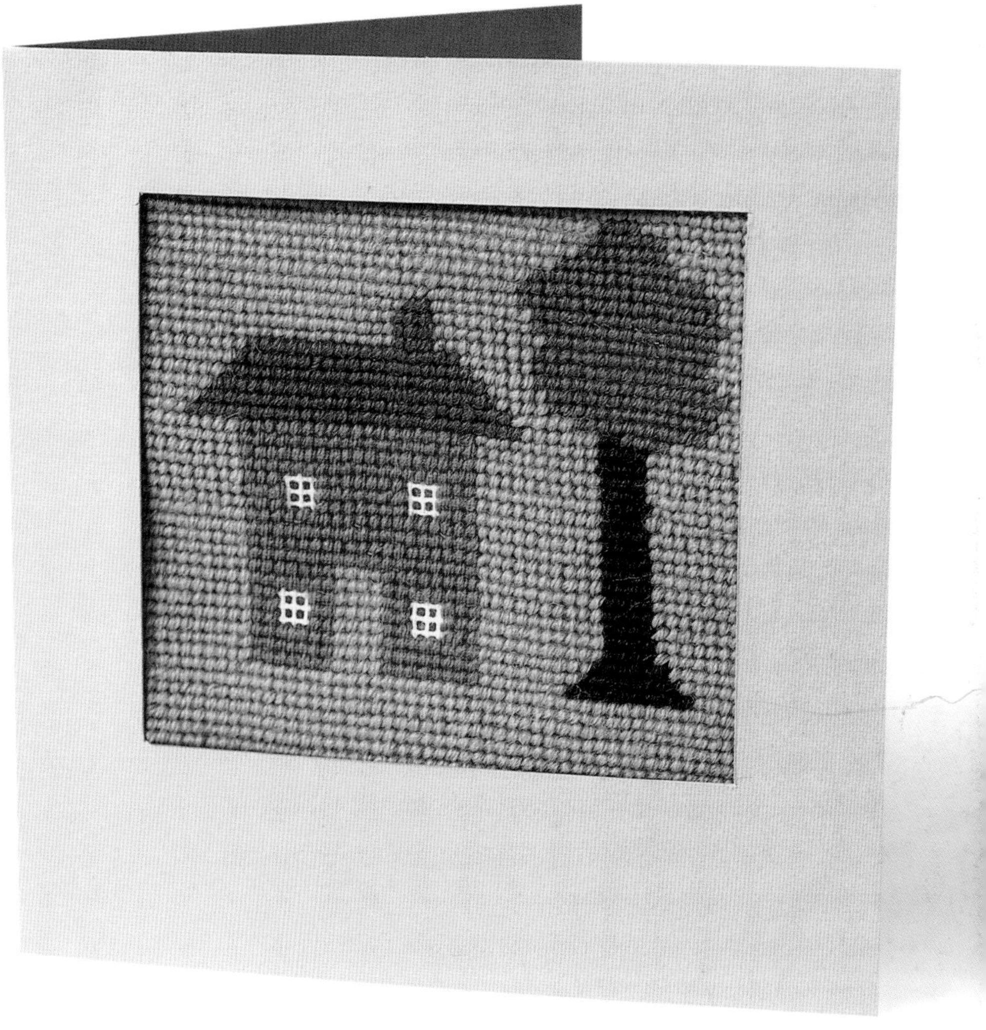

to make the **needlepoint house** card

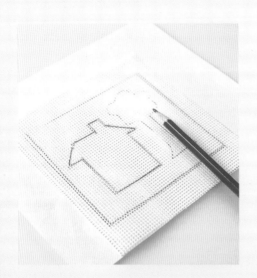

1 To transfer the design onto your canvas, first trace the outlines onto tracing paper with a dark pencil. Place the tracing under the canvas and overdraw the tracing with a pencil. Alternatively, you can count the stitches from the chart to follow the pattern.

2 Stitch the design with a classic half-cross stitch following the colour chart. Work each row from left to right, but don't stitch the windows.

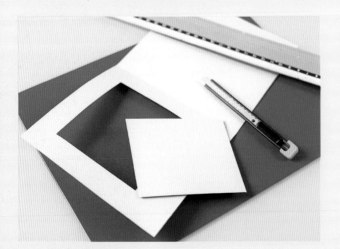

3 Fold the larger piece of blue card in half. Place the card opened out on a cutting mat and mark out the window mount to measure 10 x 9 cm (4 x 3½ in), centred 4 cm (1½ in) from the bottom of the card. Cut out with a craft knife and metal edge ruler.

4 Position the finished tapestry behind the window mount and secure in place with masking tape.

5 To conceal the back of the needlepoint, attach the smaller piece of blue card on the reverse with double-sided tape.

mother's day wire flowers

An extra special bouquet of flowers that won't need watering – perfect for Mother's Day!

materials

1 sheet of mint green card
(22 x 19 cm/8½ x 7½ in)

1 A4 sheet of thin card

1 sheet of lilac card
(8 x 8 cm/3 x 3 in)

30-cm (12-in) length of fine green wire

4 pieces of felt in different colours, such as pale pink, pink, turquoise, green
(5 x 5 cm/2 x 2 in each)

gold paper doily

button

ribbon rosebud

sequin

spray adhesive

adhesive tape

equipment

glue gun

scissors

ruler

to make the **mother's day wire flower** card

1 Fold the mint green card in half. Trace or photocopy the flower, leaf and flower pot templates onto thin card and cut out.

2 Draw around the flower and leaf templates on the reverse of the pieces of felt and the flower pot template on the lilac card and cut out the shapes.

3 Spray adhesive on a piece of gold doily and smooth it onto the flower pot. Cut away the excess.

4 Glue a button, rosebud and sequin in the centre of each of the felt flowers with a hot glue gun

5 Cut three lengths of wire each 10 cm (4 in) long and glue each one behind a flower. Glue a leaf onto each wire in a different position with a hot glue gun.

6 Decide on your flower arrangement and stick the wires to the back of the flower pot with tape at the base of the stems. Apply glue just on the reverse of the flower pot and stick on the card.

father's day photo card

Surprise your Dad with this card by sliding a dashing snap of the two of you in the frame. And for new Dads, what could be better than a photo of their little angel?

materials

1 A5 sheet of blue card
1 A4 sheet of thin card
1 A4 sheet of thin gold card
gold paper doily
1 sheet of acetate
  (21 x 10.5 cm/8¼ x 4¼ in)
spray adhesive
adhesive tape
double-sided tape

equipment

craft knife
cutting mat
pencil
scissors

(enlarge to 150% for actual size and rotate by 90° for portrait shape)

(enlarge to 150% for actual size and rotate by 90° for portrait shape)

to make the **father's day photo** card

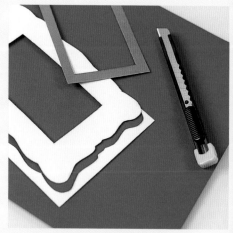

1 Fold the blue card in half. Trace or photocopy the frame templates onto thin card and cut out.

2 Draw around the frame templates on the reverse of the gold card and cut out.

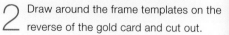

3 Cut strips of the gold doily to cover the main frame. Spray adhesive on the reverse of the pieces and smooth them in place on the frame. Cut away the excess doily.

4 Stick double-sided tape on the reverse of the inner frame and stick it in place on the main frame.

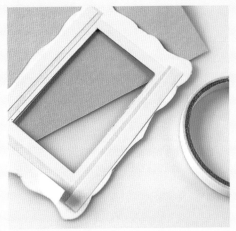

5 Attach the piece of acetate behind the inner frame with strips of adhesive tape.

6 Cut three strips of double-sided tape and stick them along the bottom and sides of the frame. Stick the frame on the card.

7 Cut your photograph to size and slide it into the frame.

champagne congratulations

With its slightly retro style, this card is perfect for sending engagement or anniversary wishes to any modern couple. Practise manipulating the metal wire before you begin.

materials

60-cm (24-in) length of thin pink metal wire plus extra for practising

pencil

1 sheet of black card (30 x 15 cm/12 x 6 in)

1 sheet of pink paper (10 x 10 cm/4 x 4 in)

strong glue

PVA glue

silver sequins

gold or silver pen

equipment

jewellery pliers

needle

eraser

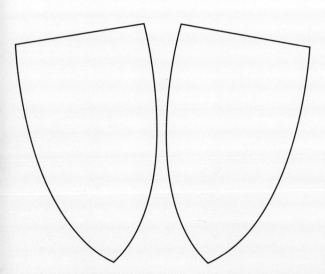

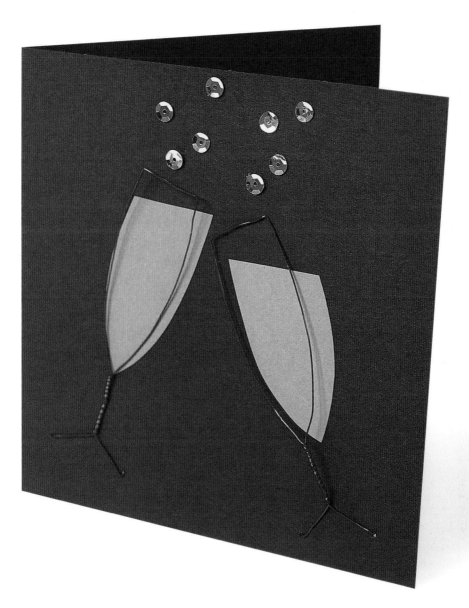

to make the **champagne congratulations** card

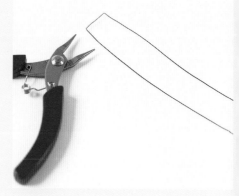

1 Cut the length of wire in half as each glass uses 30 cm (12 in) of wire. Find the centre of the wire, clamp with a pair of jewellery pliers and bend one side to 90 degrees.

2 Measure along 2 cm (¾ in) and bend another right angle to make the top of the glass.

3 Cross the wires 7 cm (2¾ in) from the top of the glass and clamp tightly with the pliers. Twist the ends of the wires to make the stem of the glass about 2 cm (¾ in) long.

4 Shape the body of the glass with your fingers. Bend each end of the wire at the base of the glass by 1.5 cm (½ in).

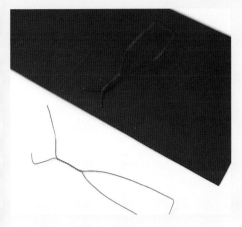

5 Fold the piece of black card in half. Position each glass on the card background and mark on the card with a pencil where the wire will be pierced through.

6 Make a small hole in the card with a needle. Pierce the wire through the holes and fold back on the inside of the card. Repeat Steps 1–6 for the second glass.

7 Cut out two glass shapes from the pink paper using the template and glue behind the glasses with PVA glue. Glue sequin champagne bubbles above the clinking glasses. Write your message inside the card with a gold or silver pen.

good luck horseshoe

Linocutting is ideal for printing multiple cards as you simply reapply the ink for each print.

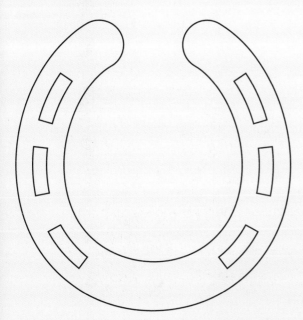

materials

tracing paper
lino board
purple water-based ink
1 sheet of whte card
  (20 x 10 cm/8 x 4 in)
1 sheet of tissue paper
  (10 x 10 cm/4 x 4 in)
fine red glitter
spray adhesive

equipment

pencil
linocutters
craft knife
piece of hardboard or glass
brayer (rubber covered roller)
rolling pin
scalloped edge scissors

to make the **goodluck horseshoe** card

1 Trace the horseshoe design onto a piece of tracing paper. Rub pencil over the reverse of the design.

2 Position the tracing paper on the lino and draw over the pattern with a pencil. This will transfer the design onto the lino.

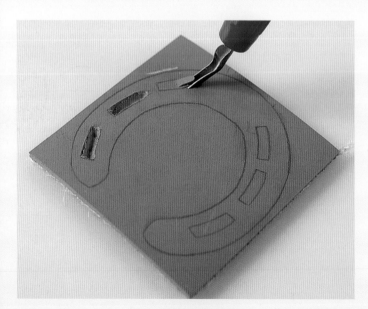

3 Warm the lino on a radiator or in the sunshine, to make scoring and cutting easier. Position the lino so that it butts up against a wall, such as the back of a kitchen work top – this will help prevent it slipping. Cut out the shape with linocutters.

4 Squeeze a small amount of ink onto a piece of hardboard or glass. Disperse the ink evenly with the roller. Run the inked roller over the linocut several times until all the raised lino is evenly covered with ink.

5 Cut a piece of tissue paper with scalloped edge scissors and lay it over the linocut. Gently smooth it in place with a rolling pin.

6 Remove the tissue paper and sprinkle glitter over the print while the ink is still wet. Shake off the excess glitter and allow to dry.

7 Fold the card in half. Spray adhesive onto the tissue paper and stick to the front of the card.

birthday

You can have lots of fun with birthday cards – pick a favourite topic or style and go to town! In this section you will find plenty of ideas for girlfriends – a stand-alone handbag, an appliqué cupcake for those with a sweet tooth, stencilled flowers and even a party dress.

handbag chic

Every woman loves a new handbag, so have fun making this for your friends using seasonal fabrics and colours you know they love to wear.

materials

2 A4 sheets of thin card

1 A4 sheet of thick white card

2 A4 sheets of thin coloured card (to match your fabric)

1 piece of flowery fabric (20 x 15 cm/8 x 6 in)

large flower sequin

ribbon rosebud

equipment

glue gun

glue brush

scissors

craft knife

ruler

pencil

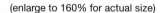

(enlarge to 160% for actual size)

to make the **handbag chic** card

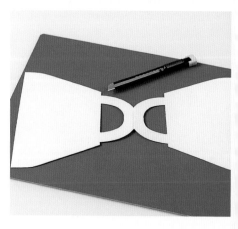

1 Photocopy the handbag template onto a thin piece of card and cut out. Fold the thick card in half. Place the top of the handbag template along the fold line and draw around the rest of the bag.

2 Cut out the handbag shape. Open it out to reveal the front and back of the card.

3 Glue the flower fabric onto a piece of paper or thin card. When the glue has dried, draw around the template, excluding the handle, onto the fabric and cut out the shape. Glue the shape onto the front of the handbag card.

4 Draw around the handle part of the template, then draw a semi-circle for the flap on the matching coloured card.

5 Glue the handle and then the flap onto the card with PVA glue.

6 Glue the sequin and rosebud onto the bag using a hot glue gun.

diamanté disco cat

This cheeky jewelled cat is sure to put a smile on anyone's face. Reduce the size of the template and use different coloured felts for a card decorated with feline friends.

materials

1 sheet of cream card
(30 x 15 cm/12 x 6 in)

1 A4 sheet of thin card

1 sheet of pale blue tracing paper (12 x 12 cm/4¾ x 4¾ in)

spray adhesive

piece of cream wool or felt
(10 x 10 cm/4 x 4 in)

4 x 9-cm (3½-in) strands of blue cotton yarn

red embroidery thread

small piece of pink felt for the nose

small piece of pink fabric for the ears

two craft eyes

6-cm (2¼-in) length of pink velvet ribbon

5 sequin jewels

equipment

scissors

glue gun

to make the **diamanté disco cat** card

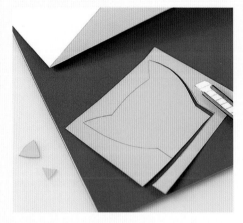

1 Fold the cream card in half. Trace or photocopy the cat, ears and nose templates onto thin card and cut out.

2 Fix the piece of blue tracing paper to the front of the card with spray adhesive.

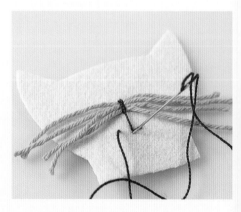

3 Cut out the cat shape from the cream wool. Position the strands of blue cotton on the face. Thread a needle with red embroidery thread and sew the yarns in place in the centre of the piece of felt.

4 Still using the red embroidery thread, sew a line 1 cm (½ in) long down from the centre of the whiskers, and a 1 cm (½ in) stitch either side to create the cat's smile.

5 Cut out the fabric for the ears and felt for the nose and glue in place with a hot glue gun, then glue on the eyes.

6 Glue the velvet ribbon for the collar at the base of the neck, tucking the raw ends on the reverse. Glue the jewels on the velvet ribbon.

7 Stick the cat to the blue tracing paper background with a hot glue gun to finish.

embroidered cupcake

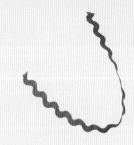

Almost edible, this is the perfect birthday card for any friend with a sweet tooth. This tasty appliqué cake is made with old scraps of fabric.

materials

1 sheet of cream card
(30 x 15 cm/12 x 6 in)

1 A4 sheet of thin card

iron-on adhesive
(15 x 15 cm/6 x 6 in)

scraps of fabric to make up the cake (see templates for sizes)

7.5-cm (3-in) length of rik-rak braid

assortment of different coloured machine threads

1 red button

spray adhesive

equipment

craft knife

cutting mat

iron

ironing board

pencil

needle

scissors

ruler

(enlarge all four templates to 200% for actual size)

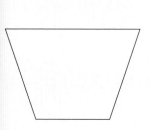

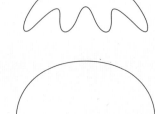

to make the **embroiderd cupcake** card

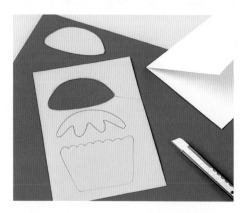

1 Fold the cream card in half. Trace or photocopy the cake and background templates onto thin card and cut out.

2 On an ironing board, iron the iron-on adhesive on the reverse of the pieces of fabric, except for the background piece.

3 Draw around the templates on the backing paper with a pencil then cut out all the shapes including the background fabric. Peel off the protective backing paper from the cupcake shapes.

4 Assemble the cupcake on the background fabric and iron in place. Start with the cake, then add the icing and the paper case. Finally, add the length of rik-rak along the top of the paper case by sewing in place with a running stitch (see page 19).

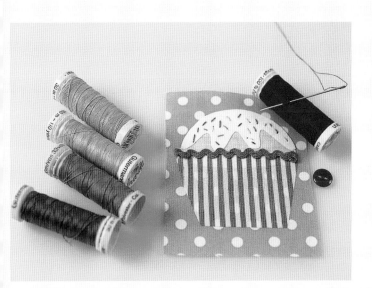

5 Embroider the small cake decorations with different coloured small stitches and sew the button on the top of the cake.

6 Sew around the casing of the cake shape with simple slip stitches (see page 19).

7 Spray adhesive on the reverse of the fabric and smooth in place on the front of the folded card.

embroidered cupcake 107

stained glass flowers

This card glows when the light shines through the coloured tissue papers. It is suitable for any occasion and could easily be adapted for a wedding or christening.

materials
sheet of tracing paper
(15 x 15 cm/6 x 6 in)
1 sheet of mint green card
(30 x 15 cm/12 x 6 in)
selection of coloured tissue
papers
PVA glue

equipment
pencil
cutting mat
craft knife or scalpel
scissors
fine glue brush
ruler
eraser

(enlarge to 130% for actual size)

to make the **stained glass flower** card

1 Trace the flower template onto a piece of tracing paper. Rub pencil over the reverse of the design.

2 Fold the green card in half. Position the tracing paper on the inside front of the mint green card and draw over the pattern with a pencil. This will transfer the design onto the card.

3 Lay the card open on a cutting mat and carefully cut out the marked design with a craft knife or scalpel.

4 Cut out small pieces of coloured tissue paper and glue them behind the flower shapes using PVA glue and a fine brush.

5 Overlap tissue paper colours and tones to create different effects, such as stripes. When the glue is dry fold the card in half.

party girl

This pretty fabric design makes the perfect card for every girlfriend or shopaholic.

materials

1 A5 sheet of white card
1 A4 sheet of thin white card
2 pieces of fabric for the dress (see templates for size)
double-sided tape
1 piece of interfacing (10.5 x 15 cm/4¼ x 6 in)
pink machine thread
butterfly sequin

Equipment

fabric marker pen
sewing machine
scissors
glue gun
pencil

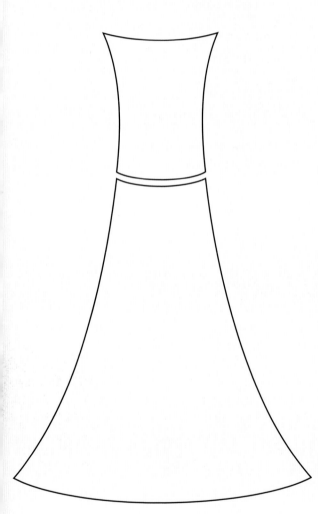

to make the **party girl** card

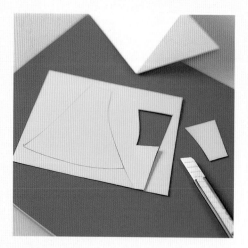

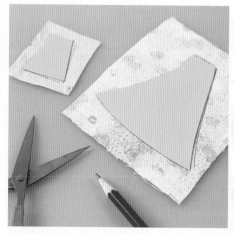

1 Fold the white card in half. Trace or photocopy the dress templates onto thin card and cut out.

2 Trace around the templates on the fabric and cut out.

3 Stick a small piece of double-sided tape in the centre of each piece.

4 Stick the dress shapes on the front of the card.

5 Place the piece of interfacing behind the dress on the inside of the card and sew around the dress with a straight running stitch, leaving approximately a 5-mm (⅛-in) border. Cut away any excess interfacing.

6 Attach the butterfly sequin to the centre of the dress with a hot glue gun and then draw a coat hanger with a pencil to finish.

butterfly surprise

This card is a two-in-one design. First, you have the flowery card and then you can turn it inside out to reveal the fluttering butterfly.

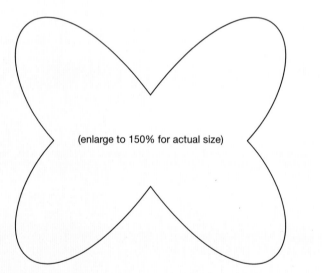

(enlarge to 150% for actual size)

materials

1 A5 sheet of pale blue card

1 A4 sheet of thin card

flowery paper, such as old
    wallpaper or wrapping
    paper

assortment of sequins

1 A5 sheet of lilac card

strong glue or glue gun

PVA glue

30-cm (12-in) length of
    5 mm (⅛ in) blue ribbon

15-cm (6-in) length of fine
    green metallic wire

2 small beads

equipment

scissors

glue brush

needle

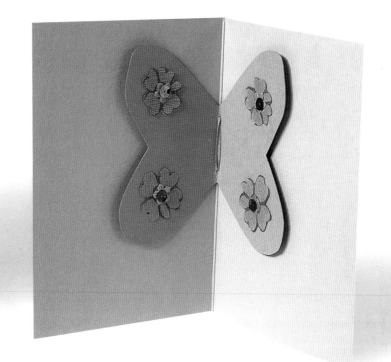

to make the **butterfly surprise** card

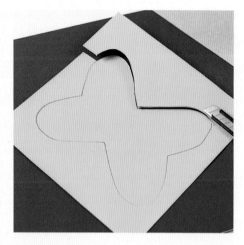

1 Fold the pale blue card in half. Trace or photocopy the butterfly template onto thin card and cut out.

2 Cut out lots of paper flowers from old wallpaper or wrapping paper. Glue two sequins onto the centre of each flower with a hot glue gun.

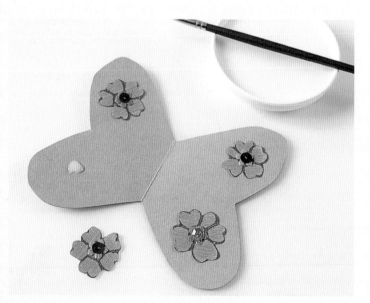

3 Trace around the butterfly template on the lilac card and cut out. Stick four of the sequin paper flowers onto the butterfly.

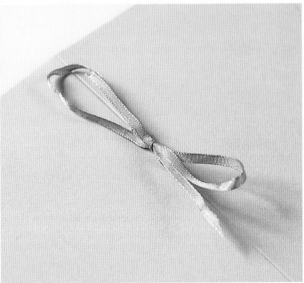

4 Thread a needle with the ribbon. Position the butterfly inside the card along the spine and sew in place with one long stitch.

5 Tie the end of the ribbon in a bow on the outside of the card and trim off the excess.

button flower

This fun flower brings to life all those wasted scraps of fabric that might otherwise have been thrown away.

materials

1 sheet of white card
  (18 x 12.5 cm/7 x 5 in)
1 A4 sheet of thin cream card
scraps of fabric
  (approximately 10 different
  patterns)
PVA glue
button

equipment

scissors
pencil
glue brush
green coloured pencil
glue gun

to make the **button flower** card

1 Fold the white card in half. Photocopy or trace the petal and leaf templates onto the thin card and cut them out.

2 Draw around the templates on the reverse of the fabrics and cut out 10 petals and 2 leaves.

3 Paint a 2-cm (¾-in) diameter circle of glue, 6 cm (2¼ in) from the top of the card. Attach the inside tips of the petals on the glue and gradually work around the circle so the petals overlap each other.

4 Glue the leaves at the bottom and draw a green pencil line approximately 9 cm (3½ in) long between the flower and the leaves.

5 Glue the button in the centre of the flower with a hot glue gun.

polka dot
present

This design lends itself to an infinite variety of colour and pattern combinations. You could also adapt the idea to make a smaller card as a matching gift tag.

materials

1 sheet of pink card
(30 x 15 cm/12 x 6 in)
75-cm (30-in) length of
stripy ribbon
double-sided tape
1 A5 sheet of red card
PVA glue

equipment

scissors
ruler
round hole punch
glue gun
glue brush

to make the **polka dot present** card

1 Fold the pink card in half and cut the ribbon into the following lengths: 1 x 15 cm (6 in), 2 x 30 cm (12 in).

2 Stick the ribbon lengths across the present with double-sided tape.

3 Tie a bow using the remaining 30-cm (12-in) length of ribbon and stick to the card with a hot glue gun where the ribbons cross over.

4 Punch lots of spots from red card and glue them onto the present in a random pattern with dabs of PVA glue.

index

acknowledgements

Executive editor: Katy Denny
Editor: Camilla Davis
Executive art editor: Leigh Jones
Designer: Lisa Tai
Photography: Peter Pugh-Cook
Production manager: Ian Paton

picture credits

Special photography:
© Octopus Publishing Group Ltd/
Peter Pugh-Cook